JABE FREDERIK

DARE TO LEAD

The Ultimate Guide to Effective Leadership,
Learn Effective Ways and Strategies on How
You Can Command People With Ease

Descrierea CIP a Bibliotecii Naționale a României
JABE FREDERIK
DARE TO LEAD. The Ultimate Guide to Effective Leadership, Learn Effective Ways and Strategics on How You Can Command People With Ease / Jabe Frederik – Bucharest: Editura My Ebook, 2021
    ISBN

JABE FREDERIK

DARE TO LEAD

The Ultimate Guide to Effective Leadership, Learn Effective Ways and Strategies on How You Can Command People With Ease

My Ebook Publishing House
Bucharest, 2021

TABLE OF CONTENTS

Foreword	7
Chapter 1: **Who is a Leader**	9
Chapter 2: **Leadership Qualities**	16
Chapter 3: **Leadership Skills**	28
Chapter 4: **The Most Effective Leadership Styles**	43
Chapter 5: **Leadership Principles**	52
Chapter 6: **Handling Opposition in your leadership** ...	59
Chapter 7: **So What Do Followers look for in their Leaders?**	65
Wrapping Up	71

FOREWORD

The Leaders Blue print is a book that was inspired by the need to develop some guidance on how an individual can enhance their influence as well as the loyalty of their followers.

It is a book that lays the infrastructure as to the strategies, principles, skills and styles which leaders could make use of. You will acknowledge that without the ability to influence people to a common goal, then the leader would not be a leader at all.

In addition, you will learn about the attributes that followers find to be admirable in leaders. These are the things that would enhance the influence and loyalty of the followers to their leaders.

The Leader's Blueprint

Command Legions Of Followers With Ease Using This Ultimate Leader's Handbook

CHAPTER 1

WHO IS A LEADER

Synopsis

This chapter examines the definition of a leader as well as the sources of power. You will acknowledge that leaders can be in either informal or formal organizations. In this case, it would be important to determine how they get to be influential to their subordinates.

In this chapter you will learn what a leader is.

What are the various forms of power that leaders can make use of?

- Coercive power
- Legitimate power
- Reward power
- Charismatic power
- Expert power

- Information power
- Referent power

Who Is A Leader?

A leader is defined as an individual who influences a group of people to act in a certain way in order to attain a certain goal. In this case, leadership is the process by which an individual enlists the support and aid of other people in an effort to accomplish a common goal or purpose. It is the creation of infrastructure for individuals to make contributions towards the attainment of a predetermined goal.

Of course there is leadership that can be defined as effective and ineffective. At this particular juncture, effective leadership would be our main concern as being in a position to influence legions of people is only desirable when it is for the right course.

Effective leadership incorporates the capacity to integrate as well as optimize successfully the use of the resources that are at your disposal whether in the internal or external environment in an effort to attain societal or organizational goals.

Standing out in the midst of many

There are many theories that abide to the aspects of leadership. It is important to acknowledge that leadership does not always have to incorporate formal authority. However, there are the unique powers that an individual must possess in order to be in a position to influence their followers or peers or even be able to control the available resources.

It is important that a leader deemed to be successful incorporate effective use of these powers in order to influence their subordinates or followers. The leaders would have to understand what the utility of power is in order to enhance the strength of their leadership.

There are various forms of powers including:

- *Coercive power* - This is power that an individual derives from their ability to offer punishment to their followers. In most cases, these powers are held by leaders in organizations in which case, they can always suspend their followers, employees or subordinates.

One thing that you can be sure of is that, as much as this power guarantees one a good following; it does not always come with love or respect. In most cases, the subordinates follow the individual not on their own will, volition or incentive but out of fear of reprisal. Many are the times that individuals are loathed when they apply this type of power to their subordinates. However, that does not undermine its utility in ensuring that the goal of an organization is attained or a quality job is done.

- *Legitimate power* - This type of power is also common within organizational structures only. In this case, an individual will only have as much power as their position in the organization, group or team allows them to. This points at the element of hierarchy in the organization as the higher the position of an individual the more the power they have.

Working together in finding solutions

- *Reward power* - Also most common in formal organizations or institutions, the power is held by a leader who has the ability to give rewards to individuals under them. In this case, they will be in a position to influence the actions of their subordinates simply because of the carrot they are floating. In most cases, these rewards are awarded to the subordinates who have performed well and could be in the form of promotions or a raise in their pay.

This has the effect of rallying the people around the same goal or purpose though in cases where the reward system is for individuals, you may have individuals pulling in different directions in an effort to outwit each other. As much as it would still get the job done, sometimes it creates conflicts when the reward infrastructure is not deemed to be fair. In this case, it could have the effect of dividing the group instead of uniting them in cases where favoritism is incorporated.

- *Charismatic power* - This power can be held by individuals in both formal and informal organizations. In this case, the ability of the leader to appeal to the feelings of their followers guarantees them instant loyalty love and even an element of fanaticism.

The leader is in a position to positively influence the followers through their charisma mainly in their speeches. The followers are able to identify with the leader creating an element of interpersonal influence. This can actually be one of the most effective powers in getting the job done. The ability of the leader to tag to the feelings of the followers confers on them a great deal of power.

- *Expert power* - This could also be in either informal or formal organizations. In this case, the individual holds a semblance of power due to their expertise, abilities, skills, experience, knowledge or abilities. A manager therefore has to be holding some expertise that other people do not have in order to remain relevant as a leader. This leader is always a valuable asset to the organization or society in which they apply their skills and expertise.

- *Information power* - This is not very different from expert power. However, the leader in this case is in possession of valuable information which would enhance the functioning of the organization or the attainment of the societal goals. One thing that you will note is that this power does not come with hierarchy as individuals in lower echelons of hierarchy could be holding more information power. This does not many it less power. In fact it is recognized as one of the most genuine forms of power as it derives its viability from knowledge.

- *Referent power* - This form of power is derived from an individual's association with another. In this case, you will have individuals going by the terms like deputy or assistant. It is not always a very dependable form of power especially as far as influencing people towards a common goal is concerned.

CHAPTER 2

LEADERSHIP QUALITIES

Synopsis

What are the qualities that an individual must be possessing in order to be in a position to influence people to a common goal? This chapter looks into some qualities and principles that a leader must incorporate in order to be effective in their leadership. It also looks at the synchronization between the individual needs and those of the company, organization or society.

In this chapter you will learn:
- Integrity
- Magnanimity
- Openness
- Dedication
- Fairness

- Humility
- Assertiveness
- Creativity
- Humor
- Visionary
- Adaptability
- Persuasion
- Training and development of your subordinates
- Cooperation and teamwork

Leadership qualities

Overview

When looking into the ability of an individual to mobilize or influence people towards a common goal, it is important that we consider the qualities that they must possess. You will acknowledge that influencing people with diverse minds, ideas likes and preferences towards a shared goal can be quite a hassle.

This is irrespective of where the authority or power of an individual is coming from. How would you synchronize your qualities with the needs of the society, organization or a group that you may be leading? You should incorporate several qualities including

1. Integrity

This quality involves the incorporation of the values and qualities not only in your words but also in your actions. This definitely breeds trust among your followers or subordinates whether in a formal organizational structure or an informal one.

This is because the followers know exactly what the leader stands for and at no one time would they expect him or her to veer off the track irrespective of the situation at hand.

There is always an element of predictability, as the leader will have their emotions well under control. This definitely does not undermine the fact that there will be objections in the course of leadership. However, being a leader with integrity means that you will be in a position to soberly solve the problem or handle the objections without tantrums or even outbursts. This makes the leader more approachable by the followers.

2. Magnanimity

This is a very essential quality in leadership. It underscores the element of taking personal responsibility when there is a failure in any aspect of the organization or group while giving due credit. In this case, the leader is in a position to thoroughly spread credit for the success all over the group in which case the followers will feel part of the success. In this case, the followers incorporate a good feeling as they feel that they are part of the solution and not the problem. This therefore has a uniting factor on all the members of the team.

3. Openness

This quality underlines the ability to listen to new ideas. In as much as they may not be conforming to the common thinking it would be important that you do away with any form of judgment and listen to any ideas that the followers may be having.

You will appreciate the fact that the new ideas may not be essential in the current times but chances are that they will be in the future. In addition, you can always derive another problem solving way from the idea. This therefore underlines the importance of being open to new ideas, as the group will always have alternatives.

4. Dedication

This incorporates the use of whatever resources that may be necessary to ensure that the job is done. In this case, the leader will dedicate their time and energy thus setting an example to the followers. You will acknowledge that since planning is a continuous process, it will be important to incorporate dedication at each and every stage of decision making. Being dedicated to the job converts challenges into opportunities availed in order to achieve the goals of the group, organization or the individual.

How much is the leader dedicated to leading by example

5. Fairness

This allows for consistency in the way in which one deals with others. This is mostly when the subordinates are on the wrong. A leader is seen to be just when they listen to all the sides of the story before making a judgment. In this case, the decision will be based on the information obtained.

In this endeavor, the leader should be in a position to deal with any follower in the same way irrespective of their relationship to them. This has the effect of awarding the leader loyalty from the followers as well as dedication to the purpose or the course of the group.

6. Humility

Humility underlines the fact that the leader is in that position not because they are better than the followers are but as an opportunity to serve and show direction. In this case, they will not be selfaggrandizing or put themselves in a position higher than all the others, but look into ways in which the others can be elevated.

This definitely has the effect of making all the followers feel good about themselves in which case it is motivating in itself in which case the followers will be more loyal to the leader.

Do you shout at your juniors when giving orders?

7. Assertiveness

This is the ability of the leader to be clear as to their expectations in order to avoid any conflicts in the future. In this case, the leader will be in a position to state clearly as well as in a firm manner the things that pertain to their goals in life.

This however imbues on the leader a responsibility of having a clear understanding of the implications of their decisions and their expectations as well as any potential challenges to their positions. This however has to be done in the right proportion as being too assertive could point at aggression while it would not be desirable to be under-assertive as far as ensuring the job is done.

8. Creativity

As leader, creativity will have to be part of your qualities as many are the times when you will be expected to think outside the box. Thinking differently ensures that you are not limited in terms of solutions even in cases where you may not be very much oriented with the subject at hand.

In this case, you will be assured of being in a position to look into issues in a manner that others may not have thought about. In most cases, this will appear to be radical as you stretch your thinking to all the possibilities.

9. Humor

As much as the leader may be approachable by the followers, there is always an element of tension even when they are talking of the most basic of issues. In this case, you could always enhance the rapport between you and the followers by incorporating humor. This has the effect of breaking the ice as well as energizing your followers. It also gives you much more control of the group as the followers can identify with you.

However, it is important to have limits as to the humor that you inculcate in your speech. Determine that the humor you incorporate does not offend anyone. Humor touching on individual's culture or body anatomy would not be desirable in the group environment as it has a high possibility of offending someone. In this case, it would be important that you also inculcate a bit of intelligence and wisdom in humoring the people.

10. Visionary

A leader is supposed to have a clear understanding as to the direction that their organization, team or group is heading. It is the vision of the organization that determines the course of action at any given time. In this case, you will acknowledge that course of action changes but not the vision of the organization.

As a leader, you will be expected to align the resources at hand and synchronize the processes in order to reach the prime goal. Where do you see yourself and the organization in the long term? You will have to frequently refer to the organization or group's vision as it sets the basis for your leadership. It is actually on the basis of the vision of the group that the people determine whether they will want to be identified with you or even the team. Vision defines the long-term goal of the organization and people will only identify with the group if there is harmony between their goals and those of the organization.

11. Adaptability

Being flexible enough to accept change in the organization is a very important quality of the leader. Rigidity determines your ability to accept failure and therefore look soberly into a problem when things deviate from their intended direction.

Given the dynamism of the modern days, you can be sure that there is no certainty in the future circumstance and therefore, you will need to take everything in your stride and be in a position to lead change. Even in times when the change is a threat to your leadership, it will be best that you take it as an opportunity to make better the organization or group instead of opposing an idea whose time has come.

12. Persuasion

Being in a position to influence others underlines the ability to persuade even those who may not hold the same views as you. There are many elements of persuasion that you would look at but to start with, you must be having a clear understanding of the situation at hand. This therefore allows you to persuade people based on facts and guided by information and knowledge. This therefore guarantees you an element of trust which comes with loyalty and dedication from your subordinates or followers. You will however acknowledge the importance of being in a position to articulate the issues at hand clearly in order to influence the people. Many are the times when people will attach some value to your opinion based on the knowledge or orientation that you exhibit towards the subject. In addition, you must underline the importance of having a good relationship with your subordinates.

13. Training and development of your subordinates

This quality relates to your ability to nurture, encourage end even enhance the capacity of your followers. It underlines the element of foregoing your needs for the sake of your follower's growth and sharing the control with them.

This looks at the element of delegating duties and offering guidance in order to develop their skills. In as much as having the same capacity as you may be a threat to your position, you will acknowledge the fact that times are dynamic and chances are the skills will be needed even when you will not be there. The need to coach people and nurture their talents in an effort to grow their capabilities would definitely draw the followers to the leader thus creating an element of loyalty.

Cooperation and teamwork

14. Cooperation and teamwork

As much as it may be your personal responsibility to oversee the operations of the group, it would be important that you acknowledge the value of cooperating with others.

The promotion of teamwork would ensure that the group is united around the same cause and purpose. The variety of skills that different individuals bring into the group or organization for the sake of obtaining a singular goal are essential for the unity as every individual feels that they are part of the solution.

No one possesses knowledge on each and every issue in the group and therefore you should know when to take the backseat especially on issues that are beyond your knowledge. Enhancing teamwork therefore means that you are in a position to be a follower in certain instances therefore enhancing the self importance of the members. It actually goes hand in hand with the ability to be magnanimous or giving due credit.

Cooperation and teamwork

15. Enhancing your relationship with the subordinates and those around you

Commanding legions of following using effective leadership would definitely demand that there be mutual respect and trust between the followers and the leader. This also undercuts the peers and even those that are related to you.

Many are the times when you will need to do a lot of networking, which definitely calls for enhanced interpersonal skills as well as communication. This also underlines the importance of being in opposition to initiate as well as deepen your relationship with the followers as this goes deeper in enhancing the goal of the organization.

CHAPTER 3

LEADERSHIP SKILLS

Synopsis

This chapter examines the skills that mark the difference between effective and ineffective leaders. There are leaders who do not succeed in uniting their followers to a particular cause while others do. Leadership demands that individuals incorporate some skills in order to keep the group focused to the goal.

What are the skills that you will need as a leader?

Every time the duties and responsibilities of a leader come under focus, one is bound to ask whether leaders are born or created through some kind of rigorous process. Being in a position to influence or to gather people around a common goal would dictate that you incorporate some skills which may not appear special but which carry a lot of weight as far as attaining your goals is concerned. In this case, it is important that you look into the following skills

At the end of this chapter, you will have learnt about:
- Obtaining as well as dissemination of information
- Skills relating to the control of the group
- Acknowledging and tapping into the group resources.
- Ability to represent the group
- Problem solving skills
- Shared decision making and problem solving
- Planning skills
- Being an example to the group

The Skills

1. Obtaining As Well As Dissemination Of Information

The importance of information in the making of decision that may be considered sound cannot be gainsaid. Relevant and factual information must be obtained for rational decisions to be incorporated in the leadership. There are various methods that you could use in this endeavor.

It would be important to acknowledge that being in a position to gather people around a common goal demand that you be in a position to communicate effectively. This is one leadership skill that cannot be compensated by any other. To begin with, you will need to be in a position to effectively communicate or exchange the information obtained and incorporate accuracy in the same. There are three aspects that are integrated in obtaining and dissemination of information.

- *To start with, you must look at the aspect of obtaining the information.* You will acknowledge that individuals are in apposition of altering or distorting information when they are giving you this information. Being in a position to look into the nonverbal behavior of the individual giving the information is definitely a prerequisite.

It is important to acknowledge that the individuals may not be obscuring the information intentionally. In this case, you may need to be careful in ensuring that you get the information correctly. To achieve this, it would be important that you ensure that your sources are credible. Credible sources will have a track record of giving information that can be relied on.

In addition, when you are getting the information from whatever source, it would be important that you be taking notes. Writing down the main information that has been obtained especially the key points ensures that you are on the right track at any time and therefore in a position to determine any discrepancies in the information.

In addition, you will need to repeat back the information that you think the person said. It is often the case that what you heard the person say is not exactly what they implied. In this case, seeking clarification on these aspects is important. It should not be lost on you that you may have misunderstood what the person said.

It is important to acknowledge that as much as you have the control over what will be heard, the sender of information controls the content, what as well as how the information is passed to you. This calls for collaboration between both of you to enhance effective communication. Giving the sender the freedom to speech is important in enhancing good communication. Show interest in what is said especially as far as new ideas are concerned. Ensure that eye contact is maintained and generally, be friendly.

- *Secondly, you will need to focus your efforts on retrieving the information.* Many are the times when you will need the information in the future. It would be important that you ensure that the information obtained is stored in manner that will not compromise its utility in the future.

There is a wide range of mediums that you could use in this endeavor. Irrespective of the medium that you choose I this case, you will need to ensure that the information is safe and will maintain its accuracy. Ease of retrieving the information should also be ensured.

- *Dissemination the information* - The information obtained and well stored will be of absolutely no use if it cannot be disseminated to those that you intend to influence as a leader. Effective communication is important in this endeavor and therefore you will need to make use of all the senses when disseminating information.

Be clear on the information, make a transition from what might appear general to specifics and use a language that can be understood by everyone. When disseminating information, it is always advisable that you encourage the communication to be two way. Ensure that you have synchronized both non-verbal and verbal communication.

2. Skills Relating To The Control Of The Group

Being in a position to gather the people around a common goal requires you to have a clear cut idea as to the purpose or direction of the group. The leader is expected to obtain equilibrium between the job getting done and ensuring cohesiveness of the group. In an effort to control the group it would be important that you ensure that you can coordinate well the particular capabilities of the individuals for the common goal. It would be important that destructive cliques are destroyed and greater participation encouraged enhancing cohesion.

When looking into this skill, you would be best placed setting the pace. This has the effect of defining the direction for the members. In this endeavor, it would be important that you do not dominate the group but ensure that you undertake proper observation and communicate with clarity. In addition, you would need to provide a framework which will allow the members to be self starters and make use of their initiative.

As a leader, you need to be very careful with the way in which you correct mistakes. Do these devoid of judgment and with respect while giving suggestions and not orders. Destructive criticism would be a definite no-no in ensuring that you have control over the group. Maintaining a humble demeanor is bound to complement these efforts while ensuring cohesiveness. Accepting responsibility in case of failure or mistakes would also be imperative.

Team building

3. Acknowledging And Tapping Into The Group Resources

For effective leadership, it would be important that you identify the resources that the group bears. These are not limited to physical resources but stretches to the skills and expertise of the members. Identify the particular skills and expertise of the members is definitely imperative.

Having their skills put to use for the common goal not only promotes the attainment of the group's purpose but also binds them to the group. You will acknowledge that this has the effect of allowing the members to identify more with the purpose of the team thus increasing their passion with the goals of the team.

Once you have recognized individual skills of every person, it would be important that you give the positions of responsibility based on that. It would be important that you b ring in activities that would enhance the recognition of individual skills, abilities and knowledge. Being in a position to draw from each other's resources enhances mutual cohesion in the group that you are leading.

4. Ability To Represent The Group

The importance of this skill cannot be gainsaid as far as rallying other people into understanding the group's ideas, purpose, feelings etc. This is exactly where effective communication comes into play. It is always important that you inculcate the ability to represent the group on a wide range of issues. Chances are that the group will at one time or the other runs into a problem. You should be able to understand the problem fully and recognize the decision that was reached upon.

Having a clear idea as to the justification for the decision and being able to articulate it is important. In this endeavor, consistency, fairness and integrity are important. You must be in a position to inculcate the ideas and feelings of all the members in order to make them feel well represented.

5. Problem Solving Skills

As stated before, problems are definitely going to crop up in the course of time. It is always important that you be in a position to solve the problems as they crop up.

This will not only have an effect of motivating those that are in your group but will also have an impact on those outside.

When looking into effectively solving problems, there are some stages that you would need to go through to ensure that you reach at a viable decision. Consider the following stages:

• *Carefully evaluate the problem* - the importance of evaluating the problem with sobriety cannot be gainsaid. You definitely will need to look at all the aspects that relate to the problem.

These include the implications of the problem on the goal of the group as well as its many facets. In this endeavor, you will need to confer with others as to the nature of the problem and reach an agreement as to the necessity of committing to tackle it. In addition, it would be important that you look at the constraints, whether external or internal as well as any support that you have.

• *The second step would be to identify the resources that are at your disposal and exactly how you could utilize them to solve the problem and come up with a viable decision.* This calls for a careful analysis of all the resources including human resources, skills, expertise and time as well as any other physical resources.

Come up with, and write down all the alternative solutions. You will understand that there is a multiplicity of solutions that would be used to resolve the problems. In this endeavor, it would be important that you determine an upper limit of the possible solutions to the problem. An upper limit is determined so as to save on time in the selection and evaluation of the possible solutions.

However, it is important that you ensure that the limit is not too low as to leave you with insufficient solutions. At this stage too, it would be important that you carefully evaluate them to determine their pros and cons. In this endeavor, it would be necessary that you incorporate all the input you can get from the team members.

This has the effect of motivating them as they feel part of the solution. From these alternatives, it would be important that you select the most viable solution. In this endeavor, you could consider the time taken in the implementation as well as any possible effects.

The problem solving procedure- coming up with a viable decision.

- *Execution of the decision* - once you have selected the most viable alternative, it would be important that you obtain the commitment of the members to the execution of the decision that is most viable. In this endeavor, it would be important that you look into the information that you gathered about individual solutions.

While this solution could have come from an individual member, it would be important that you incorporate the support and goodwill of the others t ensure that you have a viable solution.

- *Monitoring, evaluation and obtaining of feedback* - Once you have undertaken to execute the decision, it would be important to monitor its implementation to ensure that it is as smooth as possible. This also helps to arrest any possible deviations from the course of action in time to enhance smooth implementation.

While looking at evaluation, you would be looking at the achieved goals from time to time. Any deviations from the goal should be noted as early as possible and look at the underlying reasons for the deviation and how they could be changed. Changes could also be effected depending on the circumstances as well as the attained goals.

It would be important that any changes that are made in the implementation of the decisions be coming from the members to allow for more ownership of the process.

Problem solving is definitely the measure of the success of an individual as a leader. In this case, it would be important that you undertake to incorporate as much communication as possible.

Acknowledge that you cannot solve the problem as an individual without the input or support of others. In this case, it would be important that you ensure that they have the ownership of the problem solving process. This will ensure that you get the implementation done within the least possible time and using the least time.

6. Shared Decision Making And Problem Solving

To be an effective leader in the world today, it would be important that you incorporate as much input as possible. This is unlike the days gone by when authoritarian leadership was the in thing. This style of leadership has become more obsolete in facing the challenges of modern day.

In the modern day, exhibiting authoritarian leadership would point at insecurity which in itself is a weakness and not strength. It would alienate the leader as it would seem as if they are seeking to bolster their confidence or self esteem while they do not have the necessary skills. This does not undermine the fact that you need to be firm in your leadership and in the decisions that you make. It only implies that you need to inculcate he ideas of others in the decision making process and ensure that the members or everyone in the team feels that their interests are safeguarded. There are various styles that you could make use of in this endeavor. However, it is important that you acknowledge that there is no style that is universally acceptable. Every style's utility will be determined by the situation at hand as well as the context of the problem. All in all, you will need to establish the right infrastructure to ensure that group participation is encouraged as well as decision ownership.

The connectivity nature of leadership

While considering this, you must find a balance between the capability and maturity of you as an individual and that of the group.

7. Planning Skills

One thing that you will acknowledge is the continuous nature of the planning process. The main aim of planning is to enhance the attainment of the group's goal and purposes. As a leader, you will acknowledge that every decision leads to another and therefore you will need to be always on your toes as far as planning is concerned.

As pertaining to the importance of planning it forms the basis on which all the other skills are built. In fact, it is the joining factor integrating many other skills like time management, conflict resolution, problem solving, negotiation as well as performance appraisal. It helps ensure that the job is done in the right manner while keeping the group focused on the goals of the team. In addition, you will be in a better position to ensure the group remains united.

With good planning you will have improved quality of decisions as well as the options that are at your disposal at any given stage. This comes with enhanced outcome due to the quality of the information that you get as the decisions you make will be based on this. This definitely eliminates the possibility of making decision based on guesswork therefore guaranteeing that your judgment of the situations at hand is clear.

8. Being An Example To The Group

This is actually one of the most effective ways of influencing the group. It touches on transparency in both your private as well as your public life. It also means synchronizing your speech with what you do. As much as you may be in a position to make sound decisions, they must be matched with execution. Walking the talk guarantees you the people's loyalty, respect as well as love. It also ensures that the group remains together while also influencing the lives of your followers.

CHAPTER 4

THE MOST EFFECTIVE LEADERSHIP STYLES

Synopsis

This chapter examines the various ways in which leaders guide the direction of their followers whether in a formal organizational structure or an informal one. In this chapter, we will be discussing the various leadership styles and their applicability to certain situations.

You will acknowledge that some of the styles indicated in this chapter are not really applicable in most of present times' institutions. However, this does not mean that they have been deprived of their utility or that they have been rendered unimportant.

This chapter gives you an insight as to:

- Charismatic Leadership
- Transformational leadership

- Participative leadership
- Transactional leadership
- Servant leadership

The Styles

The ability of an individual to influence or mobilize the resources of an organization whether human or other physical depends on the styles that the leader uses at a particular time. An individual could influence people or determine the direction of the organization in various ways. One thing that you will acknowledge is that, with the dynamism of the present days, some of the leadership styles that were very applicable in the past may not be very effective today.

This however does not mean that the styles would not be effective in getting the job done. In fact, there are situations which would demand that a particular style be used in order to safeguard the organization or group's goal.

In this case therefore, the effectiveness of a particular style is determined by the situation at hand. The styles are actually a determinant of the organizational culture. You will acknowledge that individuals identify with an organization based on the synchronization between the organizational culture and what they consider important to them. Most of the leadership styles are related to the sources of power for the leader.

Motivation of the team makes the leadership successful

The following are the various styles of leadership:

1. Charismatic Leadership

This style of leadership is applicable whether the leadership is in formal or informal organizations. One thing that you will acknowledge is that the leader has the ability to communicate the issues that appeal to those under them or their followers. The followers actually stick close to this leader due to their admirable character. Their manner of articulation of issues enables the people to identify with them and therefore adhere to their aspirations.

At times, the leader may not have any real authority. However, they pay attention when conversing with the people thus augmenting the self-esteem of their subordinates and making them feel very important. When incorporating this style, the leader will also pay attention to the concerns and moods of their audience then use their words suitably. As earlier acknowledged, communication is one of the ways in which individuals endears themselves to others.

There are many leaders who may not have this trait naturally may develop with time. We however have to acknowledge that their followers trust them as well as become loyal to them due to their ability to take personal risks as well as acts of self-sacrifice. They are effective due to the ability of their words to persuade individuals as well as having confidence in those who are under them.

The main aspect of this style is the creation of an image in the minds of their followers as to the possibility of making the impossible happen. Their followers are actually made to feel greater in relation to others in which case, the group members seem like one of a kind. This creates a lot of unity or some kind of fanaticism. This type of leadership instills devotion from the followers as well as commitment directed to the ideological goals of the organization. Note however that their direction will be determined by the deeply seated needs and motivations of the particular leader.

Like any other style of leadership, the utility of this particular type depends on the intentions of the particular leader. It would be important that you blend charisma with an element of factualism while also remaining flexible enough to allow for proper evaluation of the sense of direction of the entire group.

In most cases, charismatic leadership comes with an element of intolerance to their challengers as well as a void of realism. This is especially when the leaders are so self absorbed and incorporate a need to be admired that their followers begin doubting their intentions.

2. Transformational leadership

This is actually one of the most effective styles of leadership. It actually incorporates an element of inspiration with the leader aiming at transforming the lives of the followers. The leader put a lot of dedication, energy, zeal and enthusiasm in getting the job done. This therefore allows for an element of passion which in most cases makes for an uplifting experience. One thing that you will acknowledge about this type of a leader is that they have a deep-seated feeling of care for their followers and therefore aim at making the conditions better to enhance their success.

The basis of this type of leadership is a vision or an insight into the future which ensures that people are converted into followers. The leader has a deep conviction about this vision and therefore selling the idea to the people would not be much of a hassle. Due to their passion in seeing things done or transformed, the leaders have the constant loyalty of their followers. They will always seize an opportunity to sell the idea to anyone willing to listen. Of particular importance is the personal integrity of the leader as this leadership style requires the trust of the followers as to the motives and intentions.

In some cases, the leader may not have a clear knowledge as to the way forward. It is important to acknowledge that there is no certainty in the course and therefore incorporating some flexibility will be essential. Being open to ideas is also very imperative as transformation demands the incorporation of new ideas.

Transformational leadership draws its inspiration from the element of leading by example showing high commitment levels to their followers.

There is a similarity between transformational leader and a charismatic one, in that both of them have to appeal to the feelings of the people through words and articulation of issues. However, you will appreciate the difference between the two in that the transformational leader has a more or less genuine concern and motivation to see full changes in the societal structures in an effort to change the lives of the followers.

It would however be important that you incorporate an element of realism in this in the vision of what can be achieved. In addition, you will need some form of insights into the particular issues pertaining to the future you see. Ensure that you do not drive the followers too hard in an effort to achieve the foreseen goal.

3. Participative leadership

This type of leader allows for greater participation of the followers in the decision making process. The effectiveness of this style is derived from the fact that people are more likely to be more committed to a course that they have designed for themselves. You will acknowledge that when people are involved in the process of decision-making, they have an enhanced understanding as to the choices they made and therefore work together to achieve the goal. Cohesion is much more enhanced in this case.

However, there are various degrees of participatory leadership. There are instances where the leader will ask for other people's opinions then make the decision themselves. In other cases, the team as a whole will reach the decision.

< Not participative				Highly participative >
A leader makes an Autocratic decision	Followers give a feedback to a leaders' proposal who then makes the decision	The leader decides on proposals of a team	A team makes the decision as equals	The team has the full responsibility in decision making

The degree by which the followers are involved in the decision making process will be determined by the decision type as well as the main goals or objectives of consultation. It would be important that the opinions of the followers are sought if and only if there is a genuine intention to consider them otherwise the subordinates may end up feeling betrayed and cynical.

4. Transactional leadership

This style derives its effectiveness from the fact that people acknowledge the rewards as well as the punishment that comes with any action they take. In this case, there are clearly established structures as to the requirements and the implications of any step taken. It is important to acknowledge that the followers must be involved in the initial stages relating to the contract guiding the engagement with issues like benefits. Being involved in deciding the terms and conditions of the contract of the engagement keeps the followers in check.

5. Servant leadership

This leadership style is very similar to transformation leadership. There is a deep-seated desire in the leader to selflessly help others to improve though the leader may not gain as much from the arrangement. In this case, the leader makes sacrifices in order for the whole society to benefit. You will however appreciate the fact that this type of leadership does not only benefit the followers but the society as a whole. This aspect draws the people to the leader.

CHAPTER 5

LEADERSHIP PRINCIPLES

Synopsis

This chapter examines the principles that a leader must incorporate in an effort to pull the human resources towards a common goal. These things keep the followers to the leader. Of particular interest is their effectiveness on the control aspect of the leader.

By the end of the chapter, you should have learnt about:

- The various principles used in enhancing the influence of a leader
- Their effectiveness in endearing the leader to the followers

The Precepts

Being in a position to influence people of diverse minds towards a common goal can be quite a hassle. There are very many diverse expectations from the followers that one is supposed to attend to. In fact, you will acknowledge that being a leader is more or less a balancing act. Despite the many challenges that an individual may meet, it is always important that they device some way to get the job done thus safeguarding their success. What are the principles that they act on?

1. Bonding principle

You will acknowledge that human beings are social animals. Effective leaders incorporate this one adage in their dealings with their followers. Being in a position to bond with the people under them allows them to offer help to others without expecting something in return. The effectiveness of this is actually more on the psychology of the followers as they identify with the leader more. Then leader appears to be one of them.

There is the unofficial loyalty that subordinates offer their seniors or leaders due to the emotional attachment. In most cases, they have the fear of losing your support or friendship. This underlines the importance of making emotional bonds like friendships at every twist and turn. In this endeavor, you could look into things that appeal to you and to the subordinates. Many are the times when the people will do something at their own volition when you have told them to do it, simply because they feel like they owe it to themselves.

2. Appeal principle

It is important to note that any person acts upon the values and beliefs that they hold dear. This is whether we are under the watch of someone or not. These are the things that tag to our hidden values. Looking into what would be appealing to the people under you is imperative for ensuring their loyalty is directed to you.

It would therefore be imperative that the goals, purposes and visions that you have be in harmony with those of the greater following. This allows the people to identify more with you. The feeling that you are one of them guarantees you an element of loyalty.

Interrelationship between the various aspects of success

3. Confidence principle

This principle is more or less related to your communication and persuasion powers. You will definitely need to be confident about the goals and visions that you are selling to the people if as all they are going to buy the idea. Confidence imbues in us an element of certainty.

This therefore underlines the fact that the mixed signals may be sent when you do not have the confidence. In most cases, confidence breeds trust as to the clarity of the direction or vision that you have for the organization, group or team. The confidence must be showing through verbal as well as non-verbal communication.

Confidence does not only have to be as pertaining to the visions that you have. Showing confidence in the skills and capabilities of the followers or subordinates has a motivating effect on them. This imbues in them a feeling of importance especially as they feel that they belong or fit where you are.

It would however be important that you establish the limits to this confidence. You need to acknowledge that overconfidence may have an arrogant look, which would have an exact opposite effect on the people.

The interrelationship between leadership, success and teamwork

4. Harmony principle

Harmony principle works on the basis of ensuring that you build on the trust that the people have through compromise. There will definitely be instances when they will put forward an argument that you do not agree with. It would be important to acknowledge that when we rebuff their arguments, they may actually end up being detached from us.

You will definitely not agree with your followers on all aspects. However, you will need to inculcate an element of passivity in order to get their trust. People only associate with individuals that they find trustworthy. Being trustworthy gives you an edge over their ability to resist your persuasion. This however calls on you to find equilibrium between their point of view and their impression on you.

5. Alignment principle

Alignment looks at the aspect of leveling everything up to remove contradictions thus eliminating any potential disagreements. This principle underlines the importance of synchronizing your speech with your actions. When your deeds are in harmony with your words kit will be very easy for the followers to trust you, as they know what to expect from you. This imbues an element of certainty in them especially when you have not been unreliable in the past.

The alignment principle also works in relation to aligning your speech and deeds with what drives or appeals to the people as pertaining to their values. You will acknowledge that aligning what you stand for with the societal expectations can be quite a tall order. However, striving towards shared or common values is always possible.

6. Pull principle

The pull principle implies creating an environment where the individuals do something out of their own volition. When people have made a decision by their own free will, incentive or volition, one thing that you can be sure of is that there will be more dedication, as they will own the process. The basis of this particular principle is the creation of a desire in the followers to make things change by changing their perception of the world and making them crave for what they do not have.

It is always easier to control people when they have made a decision out of their own volition that when you have made a decision for them. It would however be important that you have a clear understanding of not only what would be desirable to them but also how they make decisions.

CHAPTER 6

HANDLING OPPOSITION IN YOUR LEADERSHIP

Synopsis

Opposition in leadership is always expected as far as the people have diverse minds, values, goals and even motivations. This chapter tackles the ways in which you could filibuster opposition to ensure that you are not derailed from realizing your goal. In this case,

- Is it right for a leader to cross the floor to the opposition side?
- What would happen if there were still no consensus?
- What fuels opposition?
- What is the most effective way of combating opposition?

Battles

The future is always clouded with uncertainty especially in the leadership arena. When the leaders are making every effort to uplift the spirit, pride and morale of their followers or subordinates, you will acknowledge that there will always be those people or things that may derail you into loosing focus of your goal or realizing your full potential.

Is opposition bad or undesirable? Of course, it is not the best thing to happen to a leader but it could be a blessing in disguise. You will acknowledge that people have diverse minds, values and aspirations. They also have different ideas as to how they will get there, which could create conflicts, disagreements and opposition. However, the determining factor comes in the handling of opposition.

When handling opposition, you definitely have to look at the source of the opposition. You would be best placed to look at any unbecoming team dynamics or dysfunctions and ensure that you deal with them as fast as possible. The most viable solution for this is enhancing the communication structures and ensuring that there is better relationship between the team members.

It would be important to acknowledge that the team members may have worked together in the past and possibly had a bad history. This creates a form of insecurity as the team members find it more difficult to be open with each other or even freely share. You would have to make changes in the personnel as well as set an example to them. Creating a conducive environment for the reduction of the insecurity or feeling of vulnerability would also be your prerogative. It would also be important that you device a uniting factor so that all can feel like a team and not individuals.

There is also bound to be opposition from team members who are pessimistic about processes of morale building. In most cases, these team members would be a bit reluctant to throw themselves fully into the fray as they are not sure or certain about what would happen. This calls for patience and tolerance from the leader. You would also acknowledge that the people would not buy into an idea instantly. It is a process that will take time and therefore they will understand with time.

When facing opposition from a great majority

There may also be opposition from internal politics or the organizational structures. You will acknowledge that as much as changing these would be a bit of a hassle, you should not fail to try to change the structures. Acknowledge that you will never find perfect cultures in any organization and therefore working the best way you know how would be a prerogative.

Opposition can also be fueled by ambitions, agendas and the competitiveness of individuals in the team making communication very difficult. You can always sort this out by aligning the ambitions of the individuals with the goals of the organization and setting rules which would enhance more cooperation. Discouraging these behaviors would also be imperative.

Chances are that other teams will envy your dedication and the development of the team you lead. This may be driven by their desire to join your team and therefore turn into hostility to you as the leader. You can always enhance communication with the opposing side or just ignore the source, knowing well that many people would negatively respond to a success story.

Listening carefully to the opposition

Opposition is not only limited to day to day work, values, goals etc. there are times when you will need to negotiate with others on different grounds. Your dealings with others will determine how much control you have on the followers. Negotiation could also be with your team members. To start with, it would be important that the motivation behind the opposition. Is it a deliberate act to derail the process or does the opposition have a genuine concern for the welfare of the group or team?

You would have to stand back and have a clearer view of the situation. It would be important that you do not react until the opposition has been completely unclothed. Is the opposition drawing its legitimacy from your previous actions?

You would have to evaluate your view of them as this determines your body language or the response you give.

In addition, it would help to know where they are coming from, in which case, putting yourself in their shoes will be imperative to understand their point of view. This will definitely give you an idea as to the legitimacy of the concerns and enhance the quality of your response. Look into what is influencing them to act the way they are.

One of the most effective strategies of beating down the opposition is giving a new face to the problem. When you make it look as if it is a problem that is affective all of you and therefore you need to tackle by collaborating.

Many people would be open for collaboration rather than constant aggression. While on this, you would be best placed looking at the problem as a separate entity that both of you need to tackle. This has a uniting element as you incorporate your needs and theirs as well.

CHAPTER 7

SO WHAT DO FOLLOWERS LOOK FOR IN THEIR LEADERS?

Synopsis

This chapter deals with the qualities of the leaders that the followers would admire. It is more like the view of the followers about the attractive qualities of the leaders. What do they look for in leaders when deciding whom to be loyal to? In this case, you will know:

- importance of humor in leadership
- impact of pressure as well as vision on the subordinates
- importance of the leader's track record in commanding loyalty from subordinates

What Is Desired

An overview of what followers look for in leaders

As discussed in earlier chapters, there are various forms of leadership. All leaders derive their power from somewhere and therefore it is the source that determines their nature and how they lead.

One thing that you will acknowledge is that, the style of leadership that an individual takes on can be the uniting or the dividing factor as far as the followers are concerned. These qualities determine the difference in leaders from the perspective of the followers. What are the most admirable qualities of leaders from the perspective of the followers?

Making quick decision

1. **Ability to make quick decisions**

There are times that will demand speedy decisions to especially when there is a deviation from the course. How quickly can you as a leader make a decision? This however does not undermine the importance of making decisions based on facts and full information.

2. **Vision**

Being in a position to see ahead offers a challenge to the juniors and therefore there is a motivation. This especially marks the moment of achievement with excitement as the goal has been achieved. A vision more or less makes for a deviation from the normal or routine.

3. Ability to take pressure

Getting a hold of yourself even in times of anger is probably one of the most admirable traits. There will definitely be instances when you will feel like hitting the roof. However, the difference between you and others will be marked by the your ability to maintain your cool. Not showing panic when everyone else would, is definitely very admirable. It makes you look more or less infallible.

What makes leaders admirable to their subordinates?

4. Ability to listen

As much as leadership comes with the right to say and be heard, it is important to acknowledge that the subordinates have their voice pertaining to their likes and preferences. Paying attention to their voice is definitely very desirable. This could actually be the source of new and creative ideas. Listening t their voice especially in decision making safeguards their dedication as they feel like they are working on their brainchild.

5. **Track record as a winner**

Every person would like to identify with a leader who is known to be a winner. Having a history of achieving the desired goals has a reverberating effect as people have a feeling that the winning streak can be replicated even in other projects. In this case, there is an element of certainty.

6. **Does the leader care?**

This is especially as pertaining to the welfare of the followers or subordinates. Doing things that you never needed to do just to ensure that your followers are comfortable has a pull effect. Many are the time when this breeds loyalty and dedication from the juniors.

7. **Being able to push the followers to the limit of their career**

This underlines the element of nurturing growth in the career of the subordinates especially as pertaining to the training programs, imbuing values, goals and purpose in their career. It is all aimed at helping them reach the epitome of their career.

8. Incorporating humor in your dealing with them

This is aimed at relieving the tension that is there especially in the communication between the leader and the subordinate. It is actually one of the easiest ways of connecting with their juniors and has a motivating effect.

Wrapping Up

The effectiveness of a leader in the control and influence of a group is definitely a desirable aspect. There are things that set apart different leaders. There are leaders who will be termed as successful while others may not be very successful.

What are the skills, qualities, skills and principles that are applied by the successful leaders? The publication provides all these as well as the qualities that followers admire most in their leaders. You definitely do not have to wonder any more how you can handle the opposition in your organization. You can now go on and be the leader that the society needed.

Believe in your ability to bring that change in the organization, group, team or society.

Good luck.

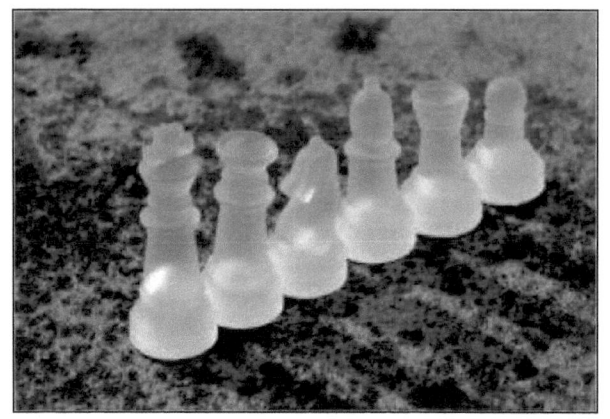

Printed by Libri Plureos GmbH in Hamburg, Germany